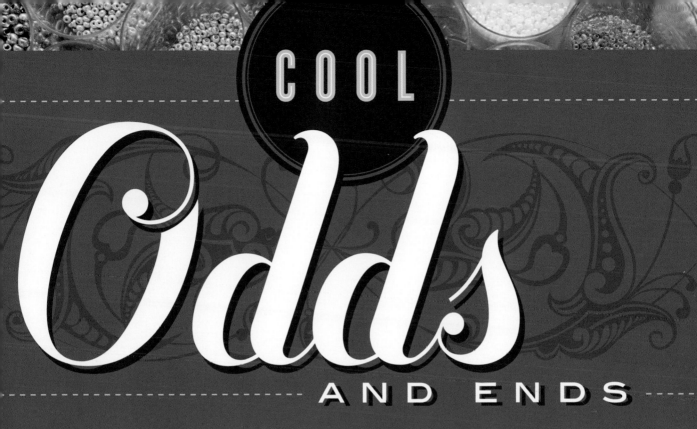

COOL

Odds

AND ENDS

PROJECTS

Creative Ways to Upcycle Your Trash into Treasure

A Division of ABDO
ABDO
Publishing Company

PAM SCHEUNEMANN

visit us at www.abdopublishing.com

Published by ABDO Publishing Company, a division of ABDO,
P.O. Box 398166, Minneapolis, Minnesota 55439. Copyright
© 2013 by Abdo Consulting Group, Inc. International
copyrights reserved in all countries. No part of this book may
be reproduced in any form without written permission from
the publisher. Checkerboard Library™ is a trademark and
logo of ABDO Publishing Company.

Printed in the United States of America, North Mankato,
Minnesota
062012
092012

 PRINTED ON RECYCLED PAPER

DESIGN AND PRODUCTION: ANDERS HANSON, MIGHTY MEDIA, INC.
SERIES EDITOR: LIZ SALZMANN
PHOTO CREDITS: SHUTTERSTOCK

The following manufacturers/names appearing in this book
are trademarks: 3M™ Scotch®, Americana® Multi-Purpose™
Sealer, Craft Smart®, DMC®, DoubleTree by Hilton™, Glitter
Glue™. Marvy® DecoColor™, Mod Podge®, NYC New York
Color®, Quick Grip™, Sanford®, Scrabble®, Sharpie®, Soft n
Crafty®, Up & Up™, Velcro®

LIBRARY OF CONGRESS CATALOGING-IN-PUBLICATION DATA

Scheunemann, Pam, 1955-
  Cool odds and ends projects : creative ways to upcycle your
trash into treasure / Pam Scheunemann.
     pages cm -- (Cool trash to treasure)
  Includes index.
  ISBN 978-1-61783-435-6
  1. Handicraft--Juvenile literature. 2. Salvage (Waste, etc.)--
Juvenile literature. I. Title.
  TT160.S2965 2012
  745.5--dc23
                              2012000132

TABLE of CONTENTS

TRASH TO Treasure

THE SKY'S THE LIMIT

The days of throwing everything in the trash are long over. Recycling has become a part of everyday life. To recycle means to use something again or to find a new use for it. By creating treasures out of trash, we are also *upcycling*. This is a term used to **describe** making useful items out of things that may have been thrown away.

Everyone has some odds and ends around the house. Perhaps something is broken, but part of it is still useful. Why not take a fresh look at all the things laying around your house and give them new life? See what you can come up with. The sky's the limit.

Permission and Safety

- Always get **permission** before making any type of craft at home.
- Ask if you can use the tools and materials needed.
- Ask for help when you need it.
- Be careful when using knives, scissors, or other sharp objects.
- Be especially careful if you happen to break any glass.

Be Prepared

- Read the entire activity before you begin.
- Make sure you have everything you need to do the project.
- Keep your work area clean and organized.
- Follow the directions carefully.
- Clean up after you are finished for the day.

Some things cannot be recycled. This includes old furniture, game pieces, wire racks, and even bowling balls! So it is even more important to look at ways to **donate** or upcycle these items.

In this book you'll find great ideas to upcycle different kinds of stuff. Make them just like they appear here or use your own ideas. You can make them for yourself or as gifts for others. These projects use easy-to-find tools and materials.

ODDS

AND ENDS

What exactly are odds and ends? The dictionary **defines** them as **miscellaneous** small items, **remnants**, or leftovers. How about that old coffee table that is scratched and has a broken leg? What about old toys you have lying around? Bits of furniture, paper, **hardware**, and plastic can be turned into some really cool things. Don't trash them, create with them!

Project Materials

Here is a list of things that could be used in upcycling projects. Think before you throw something away or recycle it. You can find ideas for upcycling almost anything. Try looking online for different projects you'd like to do.

- GAME PIECES
- PICTURE FRAMES
- METAL SCREENS
- BOWLING BALLS
- USED CDs OR DVDs
- PENCILS
- FURNITURE
- KITCHEN UTENSILS
- TIN BOXES
- OLD WINDOWS
- HARDWARE
- LEFTOVER BEADS

TOOLS & MATERIALS

ACRYLIC PAINT

ACRYLIC SEALER

ALL-PURPOSE PERMANENT ADHESIVE

COLORED WIRE

COLORFUL FLAT MARBLES

CRAFT KNIFE

DECORATIVE GEMS

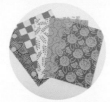

DECORATIVE PAPER

DOUBLE-SIDED TAPE

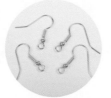

EAR WIRES

FOAM PAINTBRUSH

GLITTER GLUE

GLUE-ON BAILS

HANG RINGS

HOT GLUE GUN AND GLUE

ISOPROPYL ALCOHOL

8

JINGLE BELLS

MOD PODGE

MOD PODGE DIMENSIONAL MAGIC

OLD DOMINOES AND/OR SCRABBLE TILES

OLD FRAME WITH GLASS

OLD METAL SCREEN

OLD WOODEN RULER

PAINT PENS

PICTURE HANGERS

PILLOW STUFFING

PLIERS

STURDY STAND

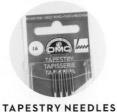

TAPESTRY NEEDLES

THIN, FLEXIBLE WIRE

WOODEN BEADS

WOODEN SKEWERS

- **OLD FRAME WITH GLASS**

- **NEWSPAPER**

- **PAINTBRUSH**

- **ACRYLIC PAINT**

- **ACRYLIC SEALER**

- **4 LARGE WOODEN BEADS**

- **WOODEN SKEWER**

- **PAINT PEN**

- **MARKER**

- **DECORATIVE PAPER**

- **SCISSORS**

- **CARDBOARD (OPTIONAL)**

- **PLIERS**

- **GLUE**

- **HOT GLUE GUN AND HOT GLUE**

FUNKY DRESSER TRAY

Keep your baubles on this beauty!

1. Remove the backing and glass from the frame. If the backing has a stand, remove it. Just bend it back and forth until it comes off.

2. Spread the newspaper over your work area. Paint one side of the frame white. Let the paint dry. Then paint the other side white. Let the paint dry.

3. Choose a color for the frame. Paint it with a few coats of that color paint. Let the paint dry between coats. Finally, add a coat of acrylic sealer.

4. Put the beads on the skewer. Paint the beads to match the frame. You may need to use a couple of coats of paint. Use a paint pen to decorate the beads. Apply acrylic sealer. Let it dry.

Continued on the next page

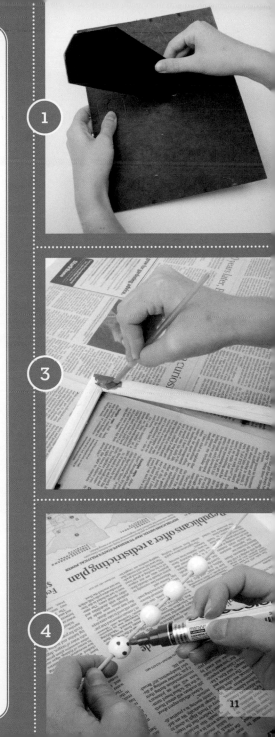

5 Trace around the glass on a piece of decorative paper. Cut it out.

6 Clean both sides of the glass. Put the glass back in the frame. Put the decorative paper face down on the glass.

7 Put the frame backing on the decorative paper. If it is loose, put some cardboard under it so it fits tightly.

Everything from photos to wallpaper can be used as decorative paper. Try using leftover wrapping paper or scrapbooking paper.

8. Secure the backing. Most frames have tabs that you push down onto the backing.

9. Cut another piece of decorative paper 1/4 inch (.6 cm) smaller than the frame. Put a thin line of glue around the edge of the paper. Press it onto the back of the frame. Let the glue dry.

10. Have an adult help you use the hot glue gun. Glue a bead to each corner of the frame. Let the glue dry.

11. Flip the tray over and set it on your dresser. Arrange your favorite **accessories** on it!

13

STUFF YOU'LL NEED

- **LARGE BASKET WITH HANDLE**
- **MEASURING TAPE**
- **PILLOW STUFFING**
- **FABRIC**
- **SCISSORS**
- **STICKY-BACK VELCRO**
- **SAFETY PINS**
- **CRAFT FELT**
- **POMPOMS**
- **TAPESTRY NEEDLE**
- **STRETCHY STRING**
- **JINGLE BELLS**

COOL KITTY BED

For first-class felines!

1. Measure the inside of the basket. Choose the fabric for the pillow. It should be 2 1/2 times longer and 10 inches (25 cm) wider than the basket.

2. Fill the bottom of the basket with pillow stuffing. Shape it into a pillow. Use enough stuffing to make it firm.

3. Cut a 4-inch (10 cm) strip of the sticky-back Velcro. Take the stuffing out of the basket. Set it in the middle of the fabric on the wrong side. Wrap the fabric around the stuffing. Remove the backing from one side of the Velcro. Stick it to the fabric where it **overlaps**. Remove the backing from the other side of the Velcro. Press the edge of the fabric onto the Velcro.

Continued on the next page

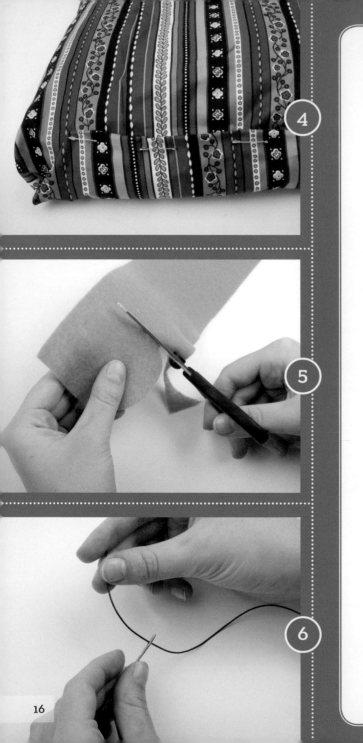

4 Fold the sides of the fabric around the stuffing like you would wrap a present. Pin the sides with safety pins. Turn the pillow over and put it in the basket. If you have a round basket, turn the corners under so it fits in the basket. Just undo the fabric when you want to wash it.

5 Now make some hanging cat toys! Cut out 5 fun shapes of felt. Try circles, triangles, squares, or rectangles. Use different colors. The shapes should be a little bigger than the pompoms.

6 Cut a piece of stretchy string about 24 inches (61 cm) long. Put one end of the string through the tapestry needle. These needles have large eyes so the string can pass through the eye. Pull through about 6 inches (15 cm) of string.

7. Push the needle through the center of a pompom. Then through a piece of felt. Repeat four times.

8. Add the jingle bell at the bottom. Run the string through the loop at the top of the bell.

9. Push the needle back through all the felt and pompoms. The string will end up back at the top pompom. Tie a double knot. The double string will make the toy sturdier.

10. Tie the ends of the string around the handle of the basket. Tie several knots. Trim the extra string. Repeat if you want to make more cat toys to hang up.

STUFF YOU'LL NEED

- **STURDY STAND**
- **BOWLING BALL**
- **ISOPROPYL ALCOHOL**
- **PAPER TOWELS**
- **ALL-PURPOSE PERMANENT ADHESIVE**
- **COLORFUL FLAT MARBLES**

GORGEOUS GAZING BALL

Add a bright spot to your garden!

1   Find a stand that will hold the ball. It could be an old metal plant stand, a stand for a vase, or even an old coffee can.

2   Place the bowling ball on the stand. Clean it thoroughly with isopropyl alcohol and paper **towels**.

3   Put a thin layer of **adhesive** on a small area of the ball.

4   Press a marble into the adhesive. Pull it back a little bit and press it onto the ball again. Do this two or three times. Then press and hold it until it stays in place. This will help the marble stick to the ball better.

5   Repeat steps 3 and 4 until the ball is completely covered with marbles.

6   The marbles will make the gazing ball very heavy. Ask an adult to help you put it in the perfect spot!

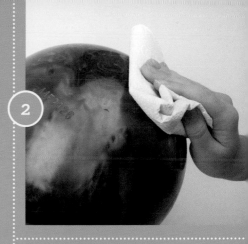

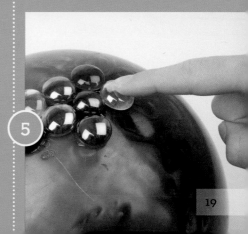

- OLD PENCILS

- PENCIL
  SHARPENER

- OLD WOODEN
  RULER

- HOT GLUE GUN
  AND HOT GLUE

- PICTURE
  HANGER

PENCIL ART

Do the write thing!

1 Sharpen the pencils until they are the length you want them to be.

2 Lay the pencils out side by side. Make sure any writing on the pencils is facing the same way.

3 Lay the ruler face up on a flat surface. Put two 2-inch (5 cm) lines of hot glue on the ruler. Have an adult help you use the hot glue gun.

4 Press the pencils into the glue while it is still hot. Add more glue as necessary. Keep adding pencils until the ruler is completely covered.

5 Glue a picture hanger to the back of the ruler. Find a place to hang your art!

21

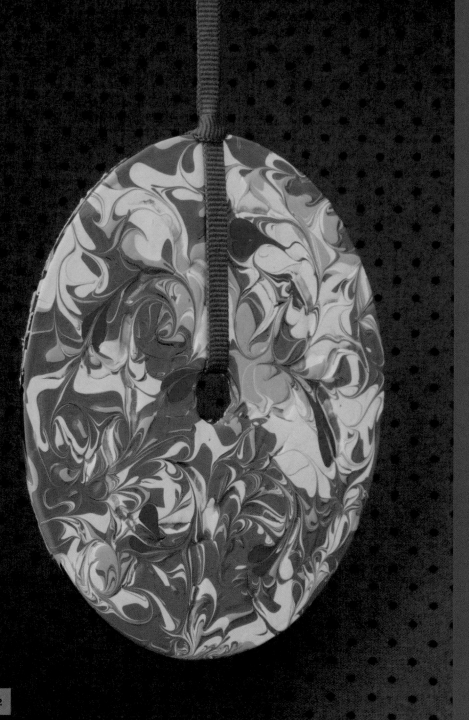

SWIRLY CD ART

An artistic way to upcycle CDs!

1   Put a couple of pieces of double-sided tape on the front of the CD. Stick it to the center of a paper plate.

2   Put some paint on the CD. Use at least three colors. Try not to get the paint too thick, but cover the surface of the CD.

3   Use a wooden skewer to make **swirls** in the paint. Be careful not to overdo it or the colors will blend together too much. Let the paint dry for at least 8 to 10 hours.

4   Put a coat of acrylic sealer over the dried paint. You may see some cracks in the paint. That's okay. Just fill them with sealer. Let the sealer dry.

5   Use a craft knife to cut around the edges and the center of the CD. Then lift it from the plate.

6   Tie a ribbon through the center hole and hang it up!

23

- OLD DOMINOES AND/OR SCRABBLE TILES

- SCRAPS OF DECORATIVE PAPER

- MARKER

- SCISSORS

- MOD PODGE

- MOD PODGE DIMENSIONAL MAGIC

- PAINTBRUSH

- GLUE-ON BAILS

- ALL-PURPOSE PERMANENT ADHESIVE

- CHAINS

- HANG RINGS AND EAR WIRES

- PLIERS

Game Piece Jewelry

No playing games with this jewelry!

1. Trace around the game piece on the decorative paper. Cut the shape out inside the lines. Trim the edges as needed to fit the game piece.

2. Brush Mod Podge on the game piece and on the back of the decorative paper. Stick the paper to the game piece. Smooth out the wrinkles.

3. Put a coat of Mod Podge on the sides and top of the game piece. Let the Mod Podge dry.

4. Cover the decorated side of the game piece with Dimensional Magic. Apply it very slowly. Try to avoid getting any bubbles in it. Pop any bubbles that appear right away. Be sure to cover the game piece all the way to the edge. Let it dry at least 8 to 10 hours.

5. Use permanent **adhesive** to glue a bail to the back. Let the glue dry and then hang it on a chain. For earrings, glue a hang ring to the back of each game piece. Let the glue dry and then use pliers to attach them to ear wires.

25

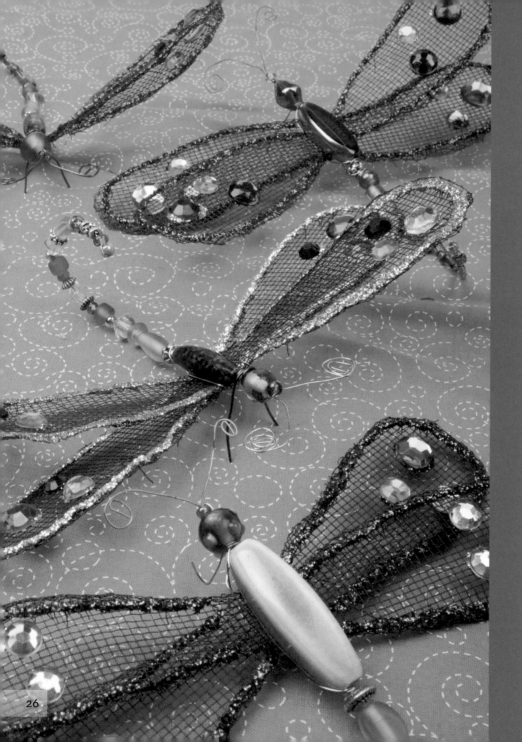

- MARKER
- PAPER
- SCISSORS
- DOUBLE-SIDED TAPE
- OLD METAL SCREEN
- PLIERS
- WAXED PAPER
- GLITTER GLUE
- DECORATIVE GEMS
- BEADS OF VARYING SIZES
- THIN, FLEXIBLE WIRE
- COLORED WIRE (OPTIONAL)
- RULER

SUPER SCREEN SAVERS

Make your old screens fly!

1   Draw dragonfly wing shapes on a piece
    of paper. The wings need to be one
    piece that is narrow in the middle. Draw
    another line 1/4 inch (.6 cm) outside
    the wing shape all the way around. Cut
    around the outer line.

2   Use double-sided tape to attach the
    paper wings to a piece of screen. Cut
    out the wings. Carefully move the paper
    wings to another piece of screen. Cut out
    a second set of wings.

3   Use a pliers to fold the edges of the
    wings 1/4 inch (.6 cm) all the way around.
    Press the edges flat with the pliers. Be
    careful! The screen can poke your skin.
    Turn the wings over and trim any stray
    wires with a scissors.

4   Set the wings on a piece of waxed paper.
    Attach decorative gems to the wings with
    glitter glue. Use quite a bit of glue, since
    some of it will go through the screen.

Continued on the next page

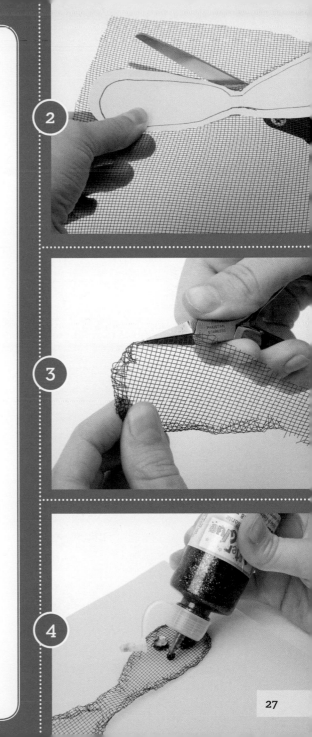

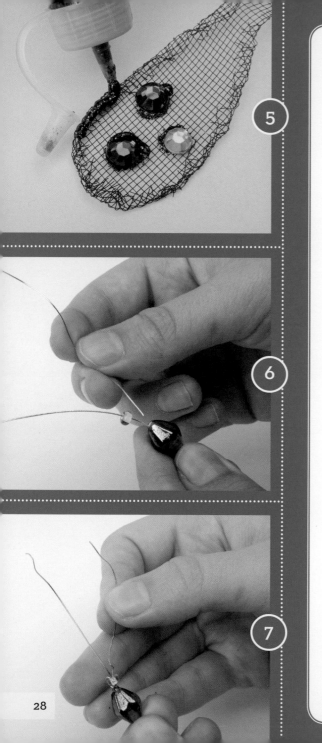

5 Put a line of glitter glue around edges of the wings. Move the wings to a clean piece of waxed paper. Let them dry completely. Then turn the wings over and add a drop of glitter glue behind each gem. Let it dry.

6 Cut a piece of wire about 24 inches (61 cm) long. Put a bead on the wire. Then add a smaller bead. Bring about 10 inches (25 cm) of the wire through the beads. Then thread the wire back through the large bead, but not the small bead. Pull it snug. This is the dragonfly's head.

7 Cut a piece of wire about 4 inches (10 cm) long for the antennae. Use colored wire if you have it. Push one end through the small bead toward the large bead. Push about half of the wire through the small bead. Wrap the antennae wire around the wire between the two beads. Then push the antennae wire back up through the small bead. Curl the ends of the antennae with a pliers.

8 Put a long, narrow bead next to the head. Put just one of the wires through the bead. This is the body. Add more smaller beads to make the tail. Stop adding beads when there is about 2 inches (5 cm) of wire left. Push the end of the wire back through the next-to-last bead. Use pliers to pull it tight. Wrap the end of the wire around the last few tail beads.

9 Cross the wings over each other at their middles. Hold them against the body bead. Wrap the remaining wire around the wings and around both ends of the body bead. Make sure the wire holds the wings on securely. Cut off any extra wire.

10 Cut a pice of wire about 3 inches (8 cm) long. Wrap it between the head and body. Make sure the ends are even. The ends can be legs if you set the dragonfly on a **shelf**. Or you can use them to hang the dragonfly on a window screen.

CONCLUSION

Now you know what upcycling is all about. What hidden gems do you have around your house? Do you have relatives who need their **attic** cleaned? What about **garage** and yard sales? Are there **thrift stores** and reuse centers near you? These are all great sources for materials that you can upcycle!

There are many benefits to upcycling. You can make some really great stuff for yourself or gifts for your family and friends. You can save useful things from going into the trash. And the best part is, you don't have to spend a lot of money doing it!

So keep your eyes and ears open for new ideas. There are many Web sites that are all about recycling and upcycling. You might find ideas on TV or in magazines. There are endless ways that you can make something beautiful and useful from **discarded** materials. Remember, the sky's the limit!

GLOSSARY

ACCESSORY – an article of jewelry or clothing that adds completeness or attractiveness to an outfit.

ADHESIVE – something used to stick things to each other.

ATTIC – a room right under the roof of a building.

DEFINE – to give the meaning of a word.

DESCRIBE – to tell about something with words or pictures.

DISCARD – to throw away.

DONATE – to give a gift in order to help others.

GARAGE – a room or building that cars are kept in. A garage sale is a sale that takes place in a garage.

HARDWARE – metal tools and supplies used to build things.

MISCELLANEOUS – of different kinds.

OVERLAP – to lie partly on top of something.

PERMISSION – when a person in charge says it's okay to do something.

REMNANT – a small bit that remains after the rest is gone.

SHELF – a thin, flat surface used to store things.

SWIRL – to whirl or to move smoothly in circles.

THRIFT STORE – a store that sells used items, especially one that is run by a charity.

TOWEL – a cloth or paper used for cleaning or drying.

Web sites

To learn more about cool craft projects, visit ABDO Publishing Company on the World Wide Web at www.abdopublishing.com. Web sites about creative ways for upcycling trash are featured on our Book Links page. These links are routinely monitored and updated to provide the most current information available.

INDEX